Eva Douglas

Francis Frith's
AROUND SOUTHPORT

PHOTOGRAPHIC MEMORIES

Francis Frith's
AROUND SOUTHPORT

◆

Clive Hardy

FRITH
BOOK CO

First published in the United Kingdom in 2000 by
Frith Book Company Ltd

British Library Cataloguing in Publication Data

Around Southport
Clive Hardy
ISBN 1-85937-106-x

Frith Book Company Ltd
Frith's Barn, Teffont,
Salisbury, Wiltshire SP3 5QP
Tel: +44 (0) 1722 716 376
Email: info@frithbook.co.uk
www.frithbook.co.uk

Printed and bound in Great Britain

CONTENTS

Francis Frith: Victorian Pioneer   7

Frith's Archive - A Unique Legacy   10

Around Southport - An Introduction   12

Around Southport   20

Out & About   67

Index   83

Free Mounted Print Voucher   87

FRANCIS FRITH: *Victorian Pioneer*

FRANCIS FRITH, Victorian founder of the world-famous photographic archive, was a complex and multitudinous man. A devout Quaker and a highly successful Victorian businessman, he was both philosophic by nature and pioneering in outlook.

By 1855 Francis Frith had already established a wholesale grocery business in Liverpool, and sold it for the astonishing sum of £200,000, which is the equivalent today of over £15,000,000. Now a multi-millionaire, he was able to indulge his passion for travel. As a child he had pored over travel books written by early explorers, and his fancy and imagination had been stirred by family holidays to the sublime mountain regions of Wales and Scotland. 'What a land of spirit-stirring and enriching scenes and places!' he had written. He was to return to these scenes of grandeur in later years to 'recapture the thousands of vivid and tender memories', but with a different purpose. Now in his thirties, and captivated by the new science of photography, Frith set out on a series of pioneering journeys to the Nile regions that occupied him from 1856 until 1860.

INTRIGUE AND ADVENTURE

He took with him on his travels a specially-designed wicker carriage that acted as both dark-room and sleeping chamber. These far-flung journeys were packed with intrigue and adventure. In his life story, written when he was sixty-three, Frith tells of being held captive by bandits, and of fighting 'an awful midnight battle to the very point of surrender with a deadly pack of hungry, wild dogs'. Sporting flowing Arab costume, Frith arrived at Akaba by camel seventy years before Lawrence, where he encountered 'desert princes and rival sheikhs, blazing with jewel-hilted swords'.

During these extraordinary adventures he was assiduously exploring the desert regions bordering the Nile and patiently recording the antiquities and peoples with his camera. He was the first photographer to venture beyond the sixth cataract. Africa was still the mysterious 'Dark Continent', and Stanley and Livingstone's historic meeting was a decade into the future. The conditions for picture taking confound belief. He laboured for hours in his wicker dark-room in the sweltering heat of the desert, while the volatile chemicals fizzed dangerously in their trays. Often he was forced to work in remote tombs and caves where conditions were cooler. Back in London he exhibited his photographs and was 'rapturously cheered' by members of the Royal Society. His reputation as a photographer was made overnight. An eminent modern historian has likened their impact on the population of the time to that on our own generation of the first photographs taken on the surface of the moon.

VENTURE OF A LIFE-TIME

Characteristically, Frith quickly spotted the opportunity to create a new business as a specialist publisher of photographs. He lived in an era of immense and sometimes violent change. For the poor in the early part of Victoria's reign work was a drudge and the hours long, and people had precious little free time to enjoy themselves.

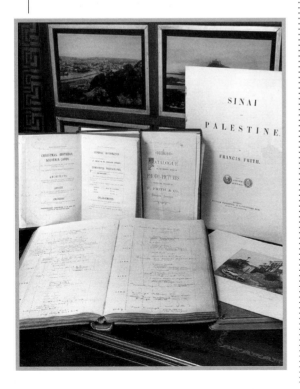

Most had no transport other than a cart or gig at their disposal, and had not travelled far beyond the boundaries of their own town or village. However, by the 1870s, the railways had threaded their way across the country, and Bank Holidays and half-day Saturdays had been made obligatory by Act of Parliament. All of a sudden the ordinary working man and his family were able to enjoy days out and see a little more of the world.

With characteristic business acumen, Francis Frith foresaw that these new tourists would enjoy having souvenirs to commemorate their days out. In 1860 he married Mary Ann Rosling and set out with the intention of photographing every city, town and village in Britain. For the next thirty years he travelled the country by train and by pony and trap, producing fine photographs of seaside resorts and beauty spots that were keenly bought by millions of Victorians. These prints were painstakingly pasted into family albums and pored over during the dark nights of winter, rekindling precious memories of summer excursions.

THE RISE OF FRITH & CO

Frith's studio was soon supplying retail shops all over the country. To meet the demand he gathered about him a small team of photographers, and published the work of independent artist-photographers of the calibre of Roger Fenton and Francis Bedford. In order to gain some understanding of the scale of Frith's business one only has to look at the catalogue issued by Frith & Co in 1886: it runs to some 670

pages, listing not only many thousands of views of the British Isles but also many photographs of most European countries, and China, Japan, the USA and Canada – note the sample page shown above from the hand-written *Frith & Co* ledgers detailing pictures taken. By 1890 Frith had created the greatest specialist photographic publishing company in the world, with over 2,000 outlets – more than the combined number that Boots and WH Smith have today! The picture on the right shows the *Frith & Co* display board at Ingleton in the Yorkshire Dales. Beautifully constructed with mahogany frame and gilt inserts, it could display up to a dozen local scenes.

POSTCARD BONANZA

◆

The ever-popular holiday postcard we know today took many years to develop. In 1870 the Post Office issued the first plain cards, with a pre-printed stamp on one face. In 1894 they allowed other publishers' cards to be sent through the mail with an attached adhesive halfpenny stamp. Demand grew rapidly, and in 1895 a new size of postcard was permitted called the court card, but there was little room for illustration. In 1899, a year after Frith's death, a new card measuring 5.5 x 3.5 inches became the standard format, but it was not until 1902 that the divided back came into being, with address and message on one face and a full-size illustration on the other. *Frith & Co* were in the vanguard of postcard development, and Frith's sons Eustace and Cyril continued their father's monumental task, expanding the number of views offered to the public and recording more and more places in Britain, as the coasts and countryside were opened up to mass travel.

Francis Frith died in 1898 at his villa in Cannes, his great project still growing. The archive he created continued in business for another seventy years. By 1970 it contained over a third of a million pictures of 7,000 cities, towns and villages. The massive photographic record Frith has left to us stands as a living monument to a special and very remarkable man.

Frith's Archive: *A Unique Legacy*

FRANCIS FRITH'S legacy to us today is of immense significance and value, for the magnificent archive of evocative photographs he created provides a unique record of change in 7,000 cities, towns and villages throughout Britain over a century and more. Frith and his fellow studio photographers revisited locations many times down the years to update their views, compiling for us an enthralling and colourful pageant of British life and character.

We tend to think of Frith's sepia views of Britain as nostalgic, for most of us use them to conjure up memories of places in our own lives with which we have family associations. It often makes us forget that to Francis Frith they were records of daily life as it was actually being lived in the cities, towns and villages of his day. The Victorian age was one of great and often bewildering change for ordinary people, and though the pictures evoke an impression of slower times, life was as busy and hectic as it is today.

We are fortunate that Frith was a photographer of the people, dedicated to recording the minutiae of everyday life. For it is this sheer wealth of visual data, the painstaking chronicle of changes in dress, transport, street layouts, buildings, housing, engineering and landscape that captivates us so much today. His remarkable images offer us a powerful link with the past and with the lives of our ancestors.

TODAY'S TECHNOLOGY

Computers have now made it possible for Frith's many thousands of images to be accessed almost instantly. In the Frith archive today, each photograph is carefully 'digitised' then stored on a CD Rom. Frith archivists can locate a single photograph amongst thousands within seconds. Views can be catalogued and sorted under a variety of categories of place and content to the immediate benefit of researchers. Inexpensive reference prints can be created for them at the touch of a mouse button, and a wide range of books and other printed materials assembled and published for a wider, more general readership - in the next twelve months over a hundred Frith local history titles will be published! The

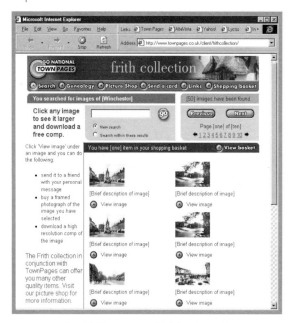

See Frith at www. frithbook.co.uk

day-to-day workings of the archive are very different from how they were in Francis Frith's time: imagine the herculean task of sorting through eleven tons of glass negatives as Frith had to do to locate a particular sequence of pictures! Yet the archive still prides itself on maintaining the same high standards of excellence laid down by Francis Frith, including the painstaking cataloguing and indexing of every view.

It is curious to reflect on how the internet now allows researchers in America and elsewhere greater instant access to the archive than Frith himself ever enjoyed. Many thousands of individual views can be called up on screen within seconds on one of the Frith internet sites, enabling people living continents away to revisit the streets of their ancestral home town, or view places in Britain where they have enjoyed holidays. Many overseas researchers welcome the chance to view special theme selections, such as transport, sports, costume and ancient monuments.

We are certain that Francis Frith would have heartily approved of these modern developments, for he himself was always working at the very limits of Victorian photographic technology.

THE VALUE OF THE ARCHIVE TODAY

Because of the benefits brought by the computer, Frith's images are increasingly studied by social historians, by researchers into genealogy and ancestry, by architects, town planners, and by teachers and schoolchildren involved in local history projects. In addition, the archive offers every one of us a unique opportunity to examine the places where we and our families have lived and worked down the years. Immensely successful in Frith's own era, the archive is now, a century and more on, entering a new phase of popularity.

THE PAST IN TUNE WITH THE FUTURE

Historians consider the Francis Frith Collection to be of prime national importance. It is the only archive of its kind remaining in private ownership and has been valued at a million pounds. However, this figure is now rapidly increasing as digital technology enables more and more people around the world to enjoy its benefits.

Francis Frith's archive is now housed in an historic timber barn in the beautiful village of Teffont in Wiltshire. Its founder would not recognize the archive office as it is today. In place of the many thousands of dusty boxes containing glass plate negatives and an all-pervading odour of photographic chemicals, there are now ranks of computer screens. He would be amazed to watch his images travelling round the world at unimaginable speeds through network and internet lines.

The archive's future is both bright and exciting. Francis Frith, with his unshakeable belief in making photographs available to the greatest number of people, would undoubtedly approve of what is being done today with his lifetime's work. His photographs, depicting our shared past, are now bringing pleasure and enlightenment to millions around the world a century and more after his death.

AROUND SOUTHPORT – *An Introduction*

A YOUNG LADY by the name of Ellen Weeton kept a diary between 1807-1825; it is one of the earliest accounts we have of what the fashionable new bathing centre of South Hawes was like at this time. Sea bathing was the latest craze for those who could afford it. A number of resorts sprang up, including Woodside (Birkenhead), Runcorn, Black Pool Town and South Hawes, and it had been the bringing of bathers to Runcorn in 1815 that had seen the first steamship enter the Mersey.

By 1825 Southport, as South Hawes was called by then, was extremely busy, and at times chaotic. Of a visit that year Ellen wrote: 'I have seldom bathed but at Southport, and there it is sadly exposing, as all who resort there well know, and the modest complain much, gentlemen's and ladies' machines standing promiscuously in the water!" What Ellen would have made of Scarborough where gentlemen were taken out into the bay by boat so that they might bathe naked we can only guess at. However, back at Southport Ellen went on to complain about the bathing machines and the lack of time allowed for getting dressed again; the owner Peter Ball banged on the door for the bathers to get out

so that the next batch could get in. Peter Ball owned about forty bathing machines, William Ball owned the hot and cold baths, whilst a Mr Dodd ran the billiard room. Bathers appear to have had a choice between three hotels: the Royal with 16 beds and stabling for 23 horses, the Union with 34 beds and stabling for 22 horses, and the Hesketh Arms with 42 beds and stabling for 39 horses.

Getting to Southport in the 1820s was by coach, carriage or cart. Though Easter was Ellen's favourite time to visit Southport, 1823 saw her divide July and August between the town and Flintshire. If travelling with her husband, the couple would come to Southport by gig, but if Ellen was on her own she would take a canal packet from Liverpool or Arpley Bridge to the Red Lion at Scarisbrick and cover the remaining five miles by cart or landau. There was also a stagecoach, the Eclipse, which ran between Southport and Liverpool via Ormskirk. During the season two coaches running alternately through Bolton and Chorley maintained a daily service with Manchester; the run took about five hours. There were carriages from the hotels to Scarisbrick Bridge to connect with boats to

Manchester, Wigan, and, of course, Liverpool.

Thomas Glazebrook was a contemporary of Ellen's, and it was he who wrote a guide to the town in 1826. Thomas wrote that in 1803 there were only thirty-eight dwellings and a population of about 100, yet by 1826 there were 215 houses and a resident population of around 600. 'In stead of a few scattered cottages, disposed according to the taste, or convenience, of the owners; - there is now a long main street, 88 yards wide, composed of handsome brick houses, with gardens in front, besides two back streets, which are rapidly forming, running parallel with the principal street'.

Prior to the advent of sea-bathing, the handful of locals had earned their livings from the sea. At the end of the 18th century there were thirteen trawl-boats, catching a variety of fish dependent upon the season, but including sole, mackerel, skate, ray, her-rings and cod, and the occasional turbot. Cockles and shrimps were taken daily, as were oysters when in season. But by 1826 the fishing was on the decline with only eight trawl-boats in regular use. The fishermen do not appear to have had any problems disposing of their catches; it became fashionable to take a boat out to meet any incoming trawl-boat so as to get the best of the fish. Though the number of trawl-boats had declined, these were offset by the appearance of pleasure craft - these were two-masted boats of 3 to 4 tonnes, each capable of carrying forty passengers.

But how did Southport the resort begin? For years there had been a tradition whereby people had come to Churchtown to take part in an event known as Big Bathing Sunday. A fair was a part of the festivities, but the highlight seems to have been to travel a mile or so to the shore at South Hawes for a bit of a paddle. In 1792 William Sutton, the landlord of

The Black Bull in Church Town, hit on the idea of building a bathing house-cum-hotel at South Hawes. Built mainly from driftwood, it stood at the end of what is now Lord Street, not far from the boundary with Birkdale. Called the Original Hotel, it closed during the winter months.

For a few years the Original Hotel was the garden to commemorate his birth. That same year, 1798, the stream running between Duke's Folly and Mrs Walmsley's house was christened the River Nile in honour of Nelson's victory.

It was at the Original Hotel that Southport is said to have got its name. The story, which has a number of variations, goes something

only substantial building at South Hawes. In 1797 Sutton replaced it with a stone building, which soon became known as Duke's Folly - Duke was Sutton's nickname, which he earned from his constant telling of the time he said that he had met the Duke of York when his grace passed through Church Town. Also in 1797 Belle Vue, the first residence, was built for a Mrs Walmsley. Others soon followed, including Beach Cottage, Willow Cottage , Belmont Cottage, and South Hill Cottage; the latter was where Admiral Ralph Barton was born. The cottage was in fact owned by Ralph's aunt, who planted a tree in like this: one night Dr Barton, a retired Ormskirk surgeon, was waving a bottle of port around when it broke, whereupon the good doctor is said to have christened the place South Port. This was a play on South Hawes; the creek (Nile), where the local fishing boats tied up and the bathers took their bracing dips into the briny; the port spilling down his person (heading south); and that the bay was once considered a safe anchorage and thereby a port. Whatever the reason the name stuck, and even Duke's Folly was eventually renamed the South Port Hotel. By 1803 the Duke was in financial difficulties, for the return on the investment needed to redevelop the Original Hotel fell far short of expectations. The Duke leased the Folly to a couple of hoteliers from Wigan, though he was imprisoned for a time for debt at Lancaster and eventually died in poverty at Churchtown.

In 1805 the town's second hotel, The Union, was built by a Mr Gass. This was also the year in which we have the first recorded use of the name South Port; it appears on a lease for a parcel of land granted to a Miss Bold. The interesting part is the wording: '... adjoining in the east to enclosed land belonging to Wm Sutton called South Port'. Does this mean that at that time only Sutton's land was officially recognised as being South Port? It took another seven years before the name appeared in the parish registers, but by 1818 it was being used on maps. By the time of Ellen Weeton's visits in the 1820s Southport was well and truly on the map. It was a time of massive investment; developers moved in, Lord Street was planned and laid down, a third inn, the Hesketh Arms was completed, and the town received its first church, Christ Church, and an Assembly Rooms.

Railway mania finally struck Southport in 1844 with proposals to build two lines, one to Ormskirk, the other to Euxton Junction. These were followed in 1845 by no less than six schemes, the West Lancashire Railway (Liverpool, Southport & Preston Junction); the Manchester & Wigan with a branch to Southport; the West Lancashire & North Union; the Liverpool, Ormskirk & Preston with a branch to Southport; the Manchester, Preston, Wigan & Southport; and the Southport & Rainford. During 1846 three proposals got as far as the House of Commons: the Grand Cross Railway (Liverpool, Southport, Preston, and Manchester & Southport); the West Lancashire (Coast Line); and the Liverpool, Ormskirk & Preston, the latter being authorised except for its proposed Southport branch. In July 1847 the West Lancashire Railway Bill was withdrawn in favour of the Liverpool, Crosby & Southport, which received its Royal Assent three weeks before the Manchester, Wigan & Southport Bill was also passed.

On 2 April 1849 the Liverpool, Ormskirk & Preston Railway opened for traffic. Passengers wishing to travel to Southport were deposited at Ormskirk, where a coach took them the rest of the way by road. Eighteen months later the Liverpool, Crosby & Southport had got as far as Sandhills from where it was possible to board direct services to Liverpool and Manchester.

On 29 December 1860 a snowstorm blocked the Southport to Liverpool line about four hundreds yards to the south of Birkdale station, trapping a passenger train. The engine was detached and the driver attempted to plough a path through the snow before reversing back onto his train. The idea was sound, but unfortunately the snow had drifted in behind the locomotive, stopping it some thirty feet short of the carriages. A relief engine from Southport could only get as far as Eastbank Street Bridge before it too became stuck. Next on the scene was a train from Liverpool, which was being double-headed by two locomotives. The leading engine was uncoupled to assist the trapped train, but was stopped short because of the snow; matters were only made worse when yet another relief engine became derailed. With no hope of moving the train, the passengers had little alternative but to scramble through the snow and seek shelter. They were led to some nearby cottages, but were refused accommodation despite the railway offering to provide coals. They then made for the Park Hotel, only to find that its heating system was frozen and the rooms damp. After a short rest at the Park, our intrepid travellers made their way on foot into Southport, where they were put up overnight in the Scarisbrick Arms and the Railway Hotel. The line was cleared the following day after being blocked for over 21 hours.

In the 1830s a German by the name of Vincenz Priessnitz began to challenge the practice of taking water treatments at spa towns by developing programmes that could use ordinary water combined with dietary regimes. Vincenz's methods gave rise to what would come to be known as the hydropathic movement; because the treatments did not rely on mineral or spa waters, hydropathic establishments could, and did, open in towns throughout the country. Southport was not immune: the Smedley Hydropathic Hotel, Birkdale Park opened in 1877 and was soon followed by The Limes Hydro, the Rockley House Hydro, and the conversion of the Palace Hotel into a hydro in 1881. Smedley also owned the hydro at Matlock, Derbyshire. John Smedley, a blunt-talking son of a hosiery manufacturer, took a trip to Cheltenham to take the treatment at a hydro. He came back full of enthusiasm and set about experimenting not only on the cows on his farm but also on some of his mill-workers. A religious fanatic with a psychotic hatred of the Church of England, Smedley combined his water treatment experiments with prayer meetings and

services using his own prayer book. His workers tolerated the treatments - after all, they were getting paid - but they drew the line at the prayers. Things appear to have worked out, because before too long strangers were turning up at the mill demanding treatments and offering to pay for them. Smedley's Hydro at Matlock opened in 1853 and was substantially enlarged in 1867 and again in 1881. Though hydros tended to be teetotal,

By 1880 Southport was the third most popular destination for the genteel end of the holiday market behind Brighton and Great Yarmouth. By 1890 there was sufficient money in the town, and the right sort of visitors, for it to support over 500 shops ranging from the early high street chains to sole trader businesses. Southport's main rival on the east coast was Scarborough; it enjoyed two seasons, a fashionable one for society, and

guests could bring their own wines, but the taking of meals tended to be a communal affair. The treatments, of which there were well over eighty, included Turkish, Russian and American baths, electro-massage, Greville Hot-Air treatment, and Nauheim treatments for affectations of the heart. Hydros tended to offer treatments all year round; in 1890 it would cost between 9s and 16s a day during the season and between 7s and 12s a day during the winter.

another for the bucket-and-spade trade. Scarborough had also attempted to be somewhat exclusive, preferring the great unwashed to go to Whitby, Bridlington and Filey - in fact, anywhere but Scarborough. There was even a move to stop the railway coming to town: Scarborough's anti-railway lobby printed a leaflet expounding the town's qualities and saying that 'the watering place has no wish for a greater influx of vagrants and those with no money to spend'. The Scarborough broadsheet was also an attack on the railways, the very mode of transport that would bring both it and Blackpool and Southport much of their wealth.

Southport's strength was its location as a residential town for Lancashire businessmen and as a place of retirement for those living off their investments, both of which influenced the town's character and development for at least seventy years. In B Bowker's book 'Lancashire under the Hammer', he relates the story of a weaver who married his boss's daughter in 1908 and went to work at the Manchester Exchange, where he sold yarn on a fixed commission rate of half a per cent. Within four years the ex-weaver had made enough money to buy a house in Southport. By 1920 he had made over £150,000 and had moved into a large house at St Annes. Lytham's development was due to the influ-

ence of the Clifton family, who owned more than 15,000 acres in south-west Lancashire, most of it having been acquired at the time of the Dissolution. St Annes was to be the last of the Fylde resorts to be developed, and would eventually be joined to Lytham, but Southport's attempt to be become a purely up-market resort never quite worked; the town relied more and more upon working-class excursionists and holidaymakers, which, of course, put it in direct competition with Blackpool. By 1871 Southport's resident population was 18,000 compared to 6000 at Blackpool. By 1881 it was 32,200 to 14,200; it was not until 1911 that Blackpool crept into the lead with a population of 58,300 against 57,600. By 1921 there was a noticeable difference with Blackpool easing into a comfortable lead at 99,600 to 76,600.

During the 1830s Blackpool, too, was still

developing along genteel lines, though it must be said that for several decades a tradition of Lancashire working people and their families visiting the town was already established, albeit on a small scale. Many would make the journey by cart, and some would even walk, just to spend a few hours away from the dust, grit, grime and monotony of mill and factory life.

By the 1870s many Lancashire cotton workers were enjoying the luxury of three unpaid days holiday a year, which, when tacked onto a weekend, gave a handy five-day break. Another important development for the holiday industry was the passing of the Bank Holidays Act in 1871. With specific days allocated for holidays, the railway companies could schedule special excursion trains, knowing that they would be filled. During Wakes Week 1919 no less that 10,000 people from Nelson stayed in Blackpool, while just 1000 headed off to Southport and around 500 went to the Isle of Man via Fleetwood.

THE WATER CHUTE 1904 52153
This photograph was taken after Easter 1904, when the Water Chute was commissioned; it soon became the main attraction at Pleasureland. Behind the right hand side of the chute can be seen the central section of the Maxim Flying Machine ride which was under construction.

THE WATER CHUTE 1904 53104
This view was taken somewhat later in the season than photograph No 52153. The Maxim Flying Machine ride is in commission, and would prove to be a crowd puller, hurtling round at 40mph. The was a similar ride at Blackpool Pleasure Beach.

THE FAIR GROUND 1913 66499

King's Gardens extended to Pleasureland. The Maxim Flying Machine is operating, and several of its gondolas can be seen whizzing round and round. Other amusements in the picture are the River Caves, a helter-skelter, and the roller-coaster. After the Flying Machine ride was dismantled part of the site was incorporated into a miniature railway.

FROM THE WATER CHUTE 1908 59933

This area of the fairground was redeveloped and incorporated into the King's Gardens, which were opened by HM King George V in 1913. The tower in the picture was at the end of an aerial ride that carried passengers over the lake; the ride was closed and dismantled at the end of the 1911 season.

KING'S GARDENS 1921 70767

The entry for Southport in one 1921 guidebook states: 'on the once lonely shore has now developed a very attractive seaside-resort and residential town, whose fine streets, notably Lord Street, challenge comparison with those of the foremost cities. The sea is continually retreating: hence the extreme length of the pier, which has an electric tramway. On the sands have been constructed marine lakes'. Of local hotels, the RAC- and AA-listed Royal (Birkdale) was the biggest, with 220 beds and garaging for 35 automobiles. The Victoria is listed as having 100 beds and garaging for 5 cars.

PLEASURELAND 1923

A view across the Promenade, tennis courts, and King's Gardens to Pleasureland. The Gardens were part of a scheme to enhance Southport's image as a garden city. In 1924 the Corporation staged the first Southport Flower Show, which soon grew to become one of the premier events of its type in the country.

◆

PETER PAN'S PLAYGROUND c1955

Depending where you came from, the ride in the middle of picture was known as a copper's helmet, and the nearest one on the left was called the nut cracker. As the nut cracker swung higher and higher the children standing on the ends had to watch out that they didn't crack their heads on the cross members.

PLEASURELAND 1923 74174

PETER PAN'S PLAYGROUND c1955 S160043

PETER PAN'S PLAYGROUND c1955 S160047
Judging from the picture, these cars were definitely big boys' toys. The cars rattled and juddered around the circuit, and on hot days there was always the pervading smell of burning oil.

THE CHILDREN'S ZOO c1955 S160056
The children's zoo was definitely a hands-on place. Here children get up close to all manner of small, and usually friendly, animals.

THE SEAFRONT 1902 48581

When the Council made it known that it was interested in acquiring the foreshore, the landowners had no objection to selling, providing the area was dedicated to recreation purposes. This led to the laying out of the Marine Gardens.

THE PROMENADE LOOKING NORTH C1960 S160155

This was the year when car ownership took off, with no fewer than 850,000 vehicles sold in the UK - an increase of 170,000 on 1959. Also, over 57,000 foreign cars were imported, which more than doubled the previous year's total. It was also the year the first Little Chef was opened.

THE PIER 1891 28558

At this date Southport had the longest pier in the country. When it opened in 1860, it was 1200 yards long and had a landing stage where steamers from the Isle of Man, North Wales, and several west-coast ports made scheduled stops during the season. Because the sea retreated, a further 260 yards had to be constructed by 1868.

THE PIER 1902 48582

Performing daily at 3.30pm and 7.30pm were the Pier Pierrots. The origins of the Pierrots go back to the London success of the mime play 'L'Enfant Prodigue', staged in 1891, and they remained in vogue right up to the outbreak of the Second World War. Pierrot troupes wore a recognisable costume consisting of a loose-fitting white silk shirt with four or five pompoms on it, a dunce's cap and white face-paint. The act included songs, mime and jokes, the members of the troupe providing their own musical accompaniment. Also appearing in 1902 were Thornley Dodge and Madame Isa Stanley; for those who liked to show off their expertise there was dancing at the Winter Gardens.

THE PIER TRAIN c1960 S160197

THE PIER TRAIN c1960

All long piers such as those at Southport, Ramsey in the Isle of Man, and Southend, were equipped with tramways, though the original idea behind them was for the conveyance of passengers, baggage, and small items of freight to and from the steamers. Some were manually worked until the 1930s, others used small steam, electric or petrol-engined locomotives. Railcars were introduced after the second world war.

THE PIER AND PAVILION 1913

The original pavilion was destroyed by fire in 1897; about five years passed before its replacement, seen here complete with minarets, was opened to the public. Appearing in 1913 were the March Hares and the White Tennessee Band - the latter could be one of the minstrel bands that did not wear black-face makeup.

THE PIER AND PAVILION 1913 66487

THE PIER 1908 59936

This picture gives us a good view of Marine Drive, built in 1894 as the sea retreated. The Drive created a large area of water around the pier, which was known locally as the Lagoon. Drainage was provided, but it proved inadequate after a very high tide, with the result that the water found its own way back to the sea by scouring out a deep channel under some of the pier supports and causing a partial collapse.

THE PIER c1955 S160114

The pavilion has lost its minarets, but it is now equipped with both an indoor snack bar and a self-service buffet. We can also see Prince's Park with its colonnade to the right of the casino. A new open-air bathing pool was added on the seaward side of the park in the late 1920s.

THE PIER ENTRANCE 1913 66486

Perhaps the man in the plus-fours and white shoes is in Southport for a spot of golf. The Southport Golf Club was formed in 1885; their course was at Marshside Hills for a few years before moving to Moss Lane. The Birkdale Golf Club was founded in 1889 as a nine-hole course in Bedford Park. Birkdale moved to its present links in the late 1890s.

THE SANDS 1902 48588
Buckets and spades, a splash and a paddle are the order of the day in this picture. The fashions of the day are interesting; both boys and girls wear blouses similar to those worn by sailors of the Royal Navy. It is also possible that the toddlers on the right are boys, as it was still the custom in some families to put young children of either sex into dresses.

THE SANDS 1908 59932
As we can see from this picture, the concept of clothes for purely leisure activities was unknown to the vast majority of people. Working people usually had one set of clothes for work and another for best, and for a trip to the seaside the best clothes came out of the closet - or the pawn shop. Many factories ran holiday clubs whereby workers could save over the year, and seaside lodgings were also cheaper if you provided your own food, which the landlady would cook.

PRINCE'S PARK BOWLING GREEN c1960 S160139
On the eve of the Great War the decision was taken to use Southport's refuse as infill for the Lagoon. The area was then landscaped and turned into a park, which was opened by the Prince of Wales in 1921.

THE MARINE LAKE 1902 48593
Here we see the North or Marine Lake about ten years after it opened. In the centre background is a windmill, which was situated on the top of the boathouse. It pumped sea water, which was used both in local water carts for street cleaning, and for flushing out the town's sewerage system.

THE LAKE 1926 79167

The South Marine Lake opened in 1887, the North Lake in 1892. For the energetic there were rowing-boats and small yachts; by this time, those wishing to take to the waters without exerting themselves could have a trip on a motorboat; it can be seen in this picture alongside the jetty.

FROM THE PIER 1908 59935

The Marine Lake covered what had been fifty acres of wet sand, which was one of the favourite haunts of sand yacht enthusiasts. Sand yachts were large four-wheeled vehicles mounting a yacht rig and capable of tearing up and down the beach at high speed. They were banned for a time after one of them collided with a bathing machine. As can be seen from the picture, the area between the lake and the Promenade was developed to provide the front with additional gardens.

THE CONVALESCENT HOME 1902 48598
Overlooking the Marine Lake was the convalescent home. It was built to take advantage of the prevailing south-westerly winds, and it reinforced Southport's claim to be a health resort.

THE BATHING POOL 1914 67465
The open-air bathing pool was a new attraction, opened in time for the long hot summer of 1914. On Sunday 28 June, as Lancashire enjoyed the hottest day of the year, an event was taking place that would set Europe aflame. In Sarajevo, Bosnia, the heir to the throne of the Austria-Hungarian Empire, Franz Ferdinand, and his wife were assassinated.

THE SANDS 1921 70766
Mums and children gather round to watch the antics of Punch and Judy, or buy an ice cream from Robinson and Eastwood's stall. The origins of Punch and Judy are in fact Italian, dating back to the Pulcinella of the commedia dell'arte, and first appeared in London in a marionette show around 1666.

THE ROYAL HOTEL AND THE WINTER GARDENS 1902 48596

The Winter Gardens opened in 1874. On the left is the concert pavilion which had seating for 2000 people, in the middle is the aquarium, and on the right is the conservatory. The concert pavilion was later used as a theatre and cinema and survived into the early 1960s; the conservatory was relegated to a roller-skating rink before being demolished in 1933.

LONDON SQUARE 1902 48601

In the 1890s there were several tramway schemes to link Southport to Lytham St Annes, though the real fly in the ointment was bridging the River Ribble. The Southport & Lytham Tramroad Co came up with a proposal to construct a transporter bridge due south of Hesketh Bank at a cost of £183,500. Though the scheme received parliamentary approval, it was never carried through, owing to problems in raising the finance.

THE MONUMENT WAR MEMORIAL 1923 74171A

Here we see the obelisk and twin colonnades of the town's war memorial in the year it was consecrated. Built in Portland stone and costing £30,000, it was one of the most impressive memorials to be built by a provincial town.

LORD STREET c1955 S160024

On the left is London Square, where the obelisk of the war memorial towers above all else. As can be seen, cars are still painted black and parking meters (being trialed in London in 1955) and 'No Waiting' yellow lines are still a few years away.

LORD STREET c1955 S160038

A member of the local constabulary is on point duty in Lord Street. The wearing of white coats was introduced in some towns during the second world war; it gave the policeman at least a sporting chance of not being run down during the blackout. There was even a plan in the 1960s to issue policemen on point duty with helmets that had a revolving flashing light on the top.

CAMBRIDGE HALL AND THE BANK 1887 20205

It was thanks to the generosity of cotton manufacturer William Atkinson that Southport got a Free Library and Art Gallery; he paid for both of them. The complex was built on a site previously occupied by a row of cottages adjacent to Cambridge Hall, and opened in 1878 having cost around £14,000. The building nearest to us is in fact the West Lancashire Bank, which opened in 1879; it was later acquired for an extension to the library.

CAMBRIDGE HALL 1902 48603

The sign above the entrance of Cambridge Hall indicates that the picture was taken around 1901-02 following the accession of King Edward VII. The Hall was opened in 1874 by Princess Mary of Cambridge for use as a place for meetings, lectures, lantern shows, recitals and so on. Further along is the Town Hall, which was built in 1854; it also housed the police court and post office.

QUEEN VICTORIA STATUE 1904 52156

Queen Victoria's statue stands in the gardens outside the Art Gallery. It was unveiled in 1904, the year this picture was taken, by the mayor, Councillor Brown. The statue was later relocated to the top of Nevill Street.

THE MUNICIPAL GARDENS 1904 52155
By this date Southport's reliance on the holiday
trade was already declining; its location made it an
attractive proposition as a residential area not only
for Lancashire businessmen and their families, but
for those living on income from investments.

THE MUNICIPAL GARDENS 1904 53105

In 1891 the resident population of Southport was 32,191 and by 1901 it had grown to over 48,000. As can be seen in this picture, a large proportion of the audience is female. At this time Southport's male population was heavily outnumbered by females. There were two main reasons: firstly, given the social make-up of the town, many families employed female servants; secondly, there were a large number of female residents who lived off income from investments, many of whom also employed female servants.

LORD STREET 1924 75785
The copper-domed bandstand was erected in 1913. During the summer season Southport was a regular venue for bands from regiments of the British Army.

THE BOULEVARD 1924 75784
This was a popular place to sit and watch the world go by. By 1924 Southport had a resident population in excess of 51,000, having grown only fractionally since 1901 when it stood at 48,000.

Lord Street Bandstand 1913 66511
The gardens were re-designed in 1911, and this copper-domed bandstand was erected in 1913. Other improvements included the provision of new lights, and the entrances were given clusters of ornate classical columns.

LORD STREET C1960 S160127

Even though there are no leaves on the trees, Lord Street is still busy; as at Blackpool, trippers visit all year round. Next to William Deacon's Bank is the Great Wall Restaurant, one of the first Chinese restaurants to open outside a major city. (It was also the first Chinese restaurant I ever went in. I was in town on a day trip from Derby with my grandmother).

LORD STREET 1887 20206

On the right is the clock tower of Cambridge Hall; the clock and chimes were paid for by William Atkinson. Beyond that is the spire of Christ Church, which had benefited from Atkinson's generosity in 1862 when he paid for the remodelling of the west front, tower and steeple.

LORD STREET 1896 37417
A horse-tram has come to a halt outside Stewart's
Bazaar and appears to be in need of some urgent
attention; the remedy seems to be a large hammer
struck against the offending part.

LORD STREET 1900 46256

The horse-tram will soon be a thing of the past. It is 1900, the same year that the system was converted to electric traction. The electric trams ran until 1934, when they were replaced by petrol buses. Other systems that closed down in 1934 were Colne, Derby, Middlesborough, Nelson, Northampton, Guernsey, Rhondda and Torquay.

LORD STREET 1891 28560

The Frith archive consists of photographs taken for possible use as a postcard. At first, postcards had to be placed inside an envelope before they could be posted, but in 1894 the rule was relaxed and they were allowed to be posted at half the normal letter rate. However, it was not until 1902 that messages could be written on them.

LORD STREET 1913 66507

Southport's residential make-up was reflected along Lord Street, where quality shops abounded. By the beginning of the 20th century the national retail chains were opening branches along what was considered one of the finest streets for shopping in England. Note the large gilt signs on the left of the picture. These had been a popular form of advertising for many years, though Thompson & Capper's sign has been modified at some time so that it can be lit up with electric lights.

LORD STREET 1913 66508

Bathchairs were once a common sight on the streets of Southport. They could be hired by the hour from the likes of John White in Shakespeare Street, or from the hydropathic establishments.

LORD STREET 1921 70775

The classical-style building on the left is the Midland Bank, claimed by many to be one of the town's finest buildings. The Corinthian columns were repeated inside the banking hall where they supported the vaulted roof. Another distinctive feature was the superb mosaic floor.

LORD STREET 1900 46255

Spot the differences between this picture and No 74166.
Some are obvious, such as the rise in popularity of
automobiles and the electrification of the tramway.
Others include the removal of the ornate cupola off one
of the buildings, the opening of the Kardomah Cafe in a
part of what had been Robson the ironmongers, and the
arrival on the scene of Malcolm Scott's.

LORD STREET 1923 74166
During the 1920s two-seater light cars made in the sports form were
becoming popular. They were easily recognisable with their polished
aluminium bodies and pointed tails, and were capable of speeds
approaching 70mph. In this picture a sporty pair zoom along Lord Street.
In the 1920s Southport, along with Blackpool, Skegness and Porthcawl,
held speed events for sports cars along the sands or the promenade, and
it was possible to tax and equip high-powered cars such as the 2-litre
Grand Prix Sunbeam for use on the roads.

LORD STREET 1923 74168

The car age has certainly arrived in Southport. Nationally, coupes and tourers outnumbered saloons by about seven to one, and they appear to being doing the same in Southport. The Prince of Wales Hotel was built on Lord Street in 1876. In the 1923 Dunlop Guide the Prince is listed has having 150 beds and garaging for 4 cars. The hotel's claim to fame is that it was the first in the country to receive RAC approval.

LORD STREET 1921 70772

Three ladies are out for a genteel stroll, though the one on the left could be about to suggest a visit to the Kardomah Cafe. To the right a couple of Boy Scouts appear to be lurking with intent to commit their good deed for the day.

LORD STREET 1902

One of Southport's double-deck tramcars rattles its way along. In 1900 the tramway took delivery of some single-deck cars known as 'Californians' on account of their American looks. In June 1920 four Southport Californians were sold to Barrow-in-Furness Corporation Tramways as a stop-gap measure until new cars ordered from Brush were delivered.

LORD STREET c1955

1955 was the first year that home sales of UK manufactured cars exceeded the 500,000 mark; imports also more than doubled to over 11,000 vehicles. It was an ideal time for Southport's motorists to invest in a new car; income tax was reduced by 6d in the pound, and waiting-lists for new cars had virtually disappeared. But in November 1955 the Chancellor suddenly increased purchase tax on new cars to 60 per cent, and restrictions on credit were brought in on hire purchase agreements - deposits of 15 per cent, and only 24 months in which to pay off the balance.

LORD STREET 1902 48605A

LORD STREET c1955 S160012

THE PALLADIUM 1914 67470
In 1914 the Palladium was offering a picture show every afternoon and George Graves & Co twice nightly. There was a time when cinema censorship was at a local level, usually performed by the watch committee. During the period of the Silver Jubilee of King George V and Queen Mary in May 1935, Southport magistrates contributed to the celebrations by allowing children under fourteen to see 'adult only' films.

LORD STREET 1896 37415
The distance between the building lines on Lord Street is 88 yds, which makes it much wider than either Union Street, Aberdeen, or the Headrow, Leeds. This is due not so much to planning, more to the history of the area. Early development needed to take into account an area of marshy ground, and in later years land for possible further development was divided into uniform rectangular plots by the landowners.

LEYLAND ARCADE 1899 43327

The Leyland Arcade has a glass roof and ornate ironwork. The arcade was the Victorian equivalent of a shopping mall, offering undercover shopping and retail outlets on two levels. In 1899 the arcade even had a bioscope parlour.

NEVILL STREET 1924 75767

Here we wee the Victoria Hotel in Nevill Street. Around the beginning of the 20th century there was little difference in the cost of accommodation at either the Victoria, the Prince of Wales, or the Royal, though eating at the latter was slightly more expensive. The Queen's and the Palace were the most expensive with rooms from 4s a night and dinner from 5s.

THE NEW INFIRMARY 1902 48599

The only medical institutions listed on the Johnson & Green street plan of 1868 are the Convalescent Home & Sea-Bathing Infirmary, and the Hydropathic Hospital. In Victorian times the provision of infirmaries depended much upon the philanthropy of a town's wealthier citizens. It was no different in Southport. The land was donated by John Ferney, a retired cotton spinner, and much of the funding was provided by William Atkinson, a cotton manufacturer.

THATCHED COTTAGES 1914 67471

In an area that once relied on agriculture and fishing, thatched cottages were once a common sight. Indeed, some of the early 'villas' built at Southport were in fact little more than up-market thatched residences. There was a group of thatched cottages at Westward and others in old Churchtown and at Birkdale.

CHURCH TOWN, BOTANIC ROAD c1955 C714044

Church Town in the parish of North Meols had long had a tradition of sea-bathing, associated with a couple of local festivals known as Big and Little Bathing Sundays, when the natives took to the waters. As with other coastal locations, Church Town began to attract visitors wishing to take the sea-air and engage in a little sea-bathing; accommodation was offered by the village's two inns, the Griffin and The Black Bull.

SCARISBRICK HALL 1896 37436

Three miles south-east of Southport, Scarisbrick Hall was remodelled by John Foster in 1814 and by Augustus Welby Pugin between 1836 and 1845. The tower was designed by Edward Pugin during a further phase of remodelling in the 1860s. The Hall was famed for its oak carvings, panelling, plaster work, and handprinted wall papers. In the front garden stood a group of stags cast in bronze and bought at auction by Charles Scarisbrick. In 1946 the Scarisbrick family sold the Hall to the Church of England for conversion into a teacher training college. In 1963 the Hall was again sold, becoming an independent school for boys.

HALSALL, THE CHURCH 1900 46259

The village of Halsall is situated near to the Leeds and Liverpool Canal. The village once had its own grammar school; the building is now the choir vestry of St Cuthbert's. The church is mainly 14th- and 15th-century and noted for its pulpit lecterns. One of these is in a sheltered position which gives the occupant the appearance of being behind bars.

AINSDALE
Street Scene c1960

Ainsdale was a failed attempt by Charles Webb to create an up-market residential area close to Birkdale. Though an independent township, Ainsdale was absorbed by Birkdale in 1903; Birkdale itself was absorbed by Southport in 1912.

◆

FRESHFIELD
Victoria Buildings c1965

Freshfield is situated between Formby and Ainsdale on the Lancashire & Yorkshire Railway route between Liverpool and Southport. In 1902 the L&Y board approved electrification of the line 630v DC; a partial electric service was to begin in March 1904, with a full service to be in place by the start of that year's holiday season. Freshfield station is still open, though it lost its goods traffic in 1968.

AINSDALE, STREET SCENE C1960 A174039

FRESHFIELD, VICTORIA BUILDINGS C1965 F117002

FRESHFIELD, THE POST OFFICE c1965 F117022
Shoppers at John Harrison's would have been paying something in the region of 6s 11d a pound for sirloin, 2s 1d for brisket, 2s 11d for streaky bacon, 4s 11d for a dozen eggs and around 3s 5d for a pound of cheese.

FRESHFIELD, RYE GROUND LANE c1965 F117001
It all looks very quiet along Rye Ground Lane, quiet enough for a group of locals to stand chatting in the middle of the road.

ORMSKIRK, AUGHTON STREET 1902 48578

An ancient market town, Ormskirk was an important centre for the linen trade during the 16th century, whilst in the late 18th and early 19th centuries there were silk mills in the area. The parish itself included the outlying villages of Bickerstaffe, Burscough, Lathom, Scarisbrick and Skelmersdale; the population of Ormskirk itself grew from 2554 in 1801 to 3838 in 1821. Over the same period the parish as a whole increased from 8251 to 12,008.

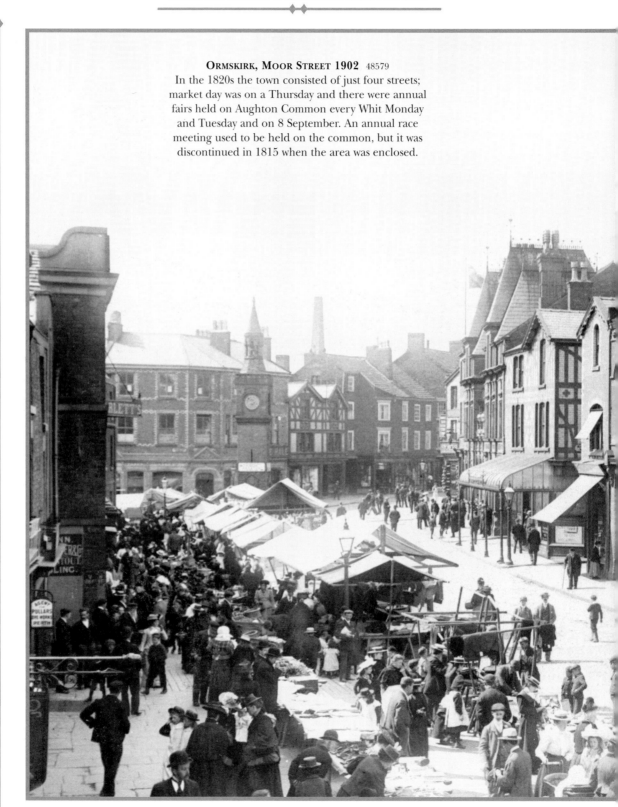

ORMSKIRK, MOOR STREET 1902 48579
In the 1820s the town consisted of just four streets;
market day was on a Thursday and there were annual
fairs held on Aughton Common every Whit Monday
and Tuesday and on 8 September. An annual race
meeting used to be held on the common, but it was
discontinued in 1815 when the area was enclosed.

ORMSKIRK, THE CLOCK TOWER c1960 O22074

There have been weekly markets at Ormskirk since 1286; the ancient market cross was replaced by this clock tower in 1876. It contains the town's fire bell, given by Lord Derby in 1684.

ORMSKIRK, MARKET PLACE 1894 34137

At this time Ormskirk was a busy little town of around 6500 people. On market days the favourite places for a tipple were the Wheatsheaf, the Talbot and the King's Arms.

ORMSKIRK, MARKET PLACE 1895 36819
As well as being a market town, Ormskirk has a long association with the Earls of Derby who lived at Knowsley Hall.
Until the Dissolution members of the family were interred at Burscough Priory; then Edward, the third Earl, had
a vault built at the south-east end of Ormskirk church.

ORMSKIRK, CHURCH STREET 1894 34138
The parish church, dedicated to St Peter and St Paul, dates from about 1276. It is unusual in that it has a separate bell tower. The explanation is that during the Dissolution the church received a peal of bells, some or all coming from the disbanded Burscough Priory. The tenor bell is inscribed 'Burscough Priory' and stamped with the dates 1497 and 1576.

FORMBY, ST PETER'S CHURCH c1960 F106040
St Peter's was built in 1739 to replace the 12th-century chapel at Raven Meols which was gradually being covered over with shifting sand. Some of the stones were salvaged and used in the construction of St Peter's. Also saved was a bell dated 1661 and a sundial. The bell turret, Gothic chancel and side chapel were added in 1873.

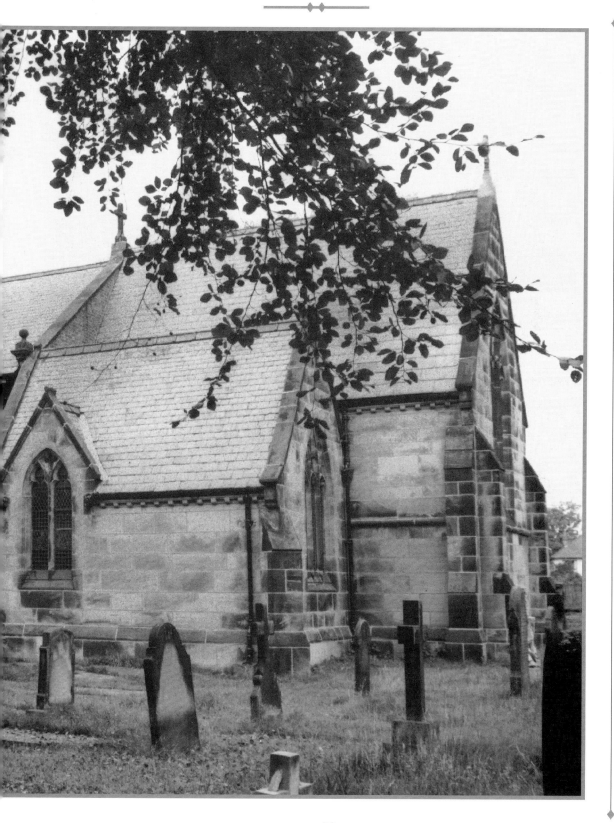

FORMBY, GORES LANE C1960 F106027
Here we see one of Formby's older properties, a fine example of the type of cottage that was once common to this part of the coast. An old custom at Formby was the carrying of a corpse three times round the Godstone in the belief that it prevented the dead from coming back to haunt their relatives. The Godstone itself is thought to date back to pagan times, being carved with a cross by early Christian missionaries.

FORMBY, TOWN CENTRE C1960 F106008
Formby was once a fishing village, but the sea has receded at a number of places along the west coast (as at Southport), leaving the town two miles inland from Formby Point. Formby owes its later development to the opening of the Liverpool-Southport railway line; this allowed the town to become a prime residential area.

FORMBY, CHAPEL LANE c1960 F106035

The coming of the railways and the subsequent growth in the town's population led to a number of new places of worship being built. The Roman Catholic Chapel pre-dates the iron horse, having been built in 1798. Later ones, however include St Luke at Raven Meols (1852-55) and Holy Trinity (1890).

FORMBY, THE POST OFFICE c1960 F106003

This view shows a peaceful scene along Brows Lane. However, redevelopment was about to rear its head. New retail outlets were built on the right hand side. They were set back from the road, and the existing pavement and shops gave way to a pull-in for about a dozen cars; several of the mature trees were also felled.

FORMBY, THE BEACH c1960 F106019

FORMBY
The Beach c1960

With room to spare, this looks as though it was an ideal place to learn the basics of driving before tempting the fates on the open road. Then again, with the sea being so far away, these vehicles might well be the forerunners of the beach buggy.

FORMBY
The Lifeboat Station c1960

For years it was believed that Bamburgh in Northumberland was the world's first lifeboat station when a converted coble was placed there in 1786. In the 1970s evidence was unearthed that as early as March 1777 the authorities in Liverpool had given orders for repairs to 'the boat, which was formerly ordered to be built and kept at Formby in readiness to fetch any shipwrecked persons from the banks'. However, the sands gradually began to engulf the station, and it was closed down in 1919.

FORMBY, THE LIFEBOAT STATION c1960 F106030

Index

The Bank 44
The Bathing Pool 39
The Boulevard 49
Cambridge Hall 44, 45
Convalesent Home 39
Fair Ground 21
Kings Garden 22
Leyland Arcade 65
London Square 42
Lord Street 43, 44, 49, 50, 51, 52–53, 54–55, 56, 57, 58–59, 60–61, 62, 63, 64
Marine Drive 31
Marine Lake 37, 38
Municipal Gardens 46–47, 48, 50
Nevill Street 65
New Infirmary 66
Palladium 64
Pavillion 30, 31, 32–33, 34–35, 36
Peter Pans Playground 23, 24
The Pier 26–27, 28–29, 30, 31, 32–33, 34–35,36
Pleasureland 23
Princes Park 37
Promenade 25, 38
Queen Victoria Statue 45
Royal Hotel 42
Sands 34–35, 36, 40–41
Seafront 25
Thatched Cottages 66
Town Hall 45
War Memorial 43
Water Chute 20, 21
Winter Gardens 42
Zoo 24

Out & About
Ainsdale 69
Church Town 67
Formby 78–79, 80, 81, 82
Freshfield 69, 70
Halsall 68
Ormskirk 71, 72–73, 74, 75, 76–77
Scarisbrick Hall 67

Frith Book Co Titles

Frith Book Company publish over a 100 new titles each year. For latest catalogue please contact Frith Book Co

Town Books 96pp, 100 photos. County and Themed Books 128pp, 150 photos
(unless specified) All titles hardback laminated case and jacket
except those indicated pb (paperback)

Around Barnstaple	1-85937-084-5	£12.99
Around Blackpool	1-85937-049-7	£12.99
Around Bognor Regis	1-85937-055-1	£12.99
Around Bristol	1-85937-050-0	£12.99
Around Cambridge	1-85937-092-6	£12.99
Cheshire	1-85937-045-4	£14.99
Around Chester	1-85937-090-X	£12.99
Around Chesterfield	1-85937-071-3	£12.99

Around Maidstone	1-85937-056-X	£12.99
North Yorkshire	1-85937-048-9	£14.99
Around Nottingham	1-85937-060-8	£12.99
Around Penzance	1-85937-069-1	£12.99
Around Reading	1-85937-087-X	£12.99
Around St Ives	1-85937-068-3	£12.99
Around Salisbury	1-85937-091-8	£12.99
Around Scarborough	1-85937-104-3	£12.99
Scottish Castles	1-85937-077-2	£14.99
Around Sevenoaks and Tonbridge	1-85937-057-8	£12.99
Sheffield and S Yorkshire	1-85937-070-5	£14.99
Shropshire	1-85937-083-7	£14.99
Staffordshire	1-85937-047-0 (96pp)	£12.99
Suffolk	1-85937-074-8	£14.99
Surrey	1-85937-081-0	£14.99
Torbay	1-85937-063-2	£12.99
Wiltshire	1-85937-053-5	£14.99

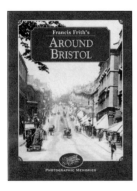 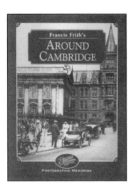

Around Chichester	1-85937-089-6	£12.99
Cornwall	1-85937-054-3	£14.99
Cotswolds	1-85937-099-3	£14.99
Around Derby	1-85937-046-2	£12.99
Devon	1-85937-052-7	£14.99
Dorset	1-85937-075-6	£14.99
Dorset Coast	1-85937-062-4	£14.99
Around Dublin	1-85937-058-6	£12.99
East Anglia	1-85937-059-4	£14.99
Around Eastbourne	1-85937-061-6	£12.99
English Castles	1-85937-078-0	£14.99
Around Falmouth	1-85937-066-7	£12.99
Hampshire	1-85937-064-0	£14.99
Isle of Man	1-85937-065-9	£14.99

British Life A Century Ago
246 x 189mm 144pp, hardback. Black and white Lavishly illustrated with photos from the turn of the century, and with extensive commentary. It offers a unique insight into the social history and heritage of bygone Britain.

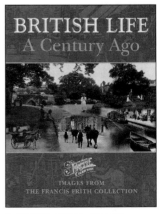

1-85937-103-5 £17.99

Available from your local bookshop or from the publisher

Frith Book Co Titles Available in 2000

Around Bakewell	1-85937-1132	£12.99	Feb
Around Bath	1-85937-097-7	£12.99	Feb
Around Belfast	1-85937-094-2	£12.99	Feb
Around Bournemouth	1-85937-067-5	£12.99	Feb
Cambridgeshire	1-85937-086-1	£14.99	Feb
Essex	1-85937-082-9	£14.99	Feb
Greater Manchester	1-85937-108-6	£14.99	Feb
Around Guildford	1-85937-117-5	£12.99	Feb
Around Harrogate	1-85937-112-4	£12.99	Feb
Hertfordshire	1-85937-079-9	£14.99	Feb
Isle of Wight	1-85937-114-0	£14.99	Feb
Around Lincoln	1-85937-111-6	£12.99	Feb
Margate/Ramsgate	1-85937-116-7	£12.99	Feb
Northumberland and Tyne & Wear			
	1-85937-072-1	£14.99	Feb
Around Newark	1-85937-105-1	£12.99	Feb
Around Oxford	1-85937-096-9	£12.99	Feb
Oxfordshire	1-85937-076-4	£14.99	Feb
Around Shrewsbury	1-85937-110-8	£12.99	Feb
South Devon Coast	1-85937-107-8	£14.99	Feb
Around Southport	1-85937-106-x	£12.99	Feb
West Midlands	1-85937-109-4	£14.99	Feb
Cambridgeshire	1-85937-086-1	£14.99	Mar
County Durham	1-85937-123-x	£14.99	Mar
Cumbria	1-85937-101-9	£14.99	Mar
Down the Severn	1-85937-118-3	£14.99	Mar
Down the Thames	1-85937-121-3	£14.99	Mar
Around Exeter	1-85937-126-4	£12.99	Mar
Around Folkestone	1-85937-124-8	£12.99	Mar
Gloucestershire	1-85937-102-7	£14.99	Mar
Around Great Yarmouth			
	1-85937-085-3	£12.99	Mar
Kent Living Memories	1-85937-125-6	£14.99	Mar
Around Leicester	1-85937-073-x	£12.99	Mar
Around Liverpool	1-85937-051-9	£12.99	Mar
Around Plymouth	1-85937-119-1	£12.99	Mar
Around Portsmouth	1-85937-122-1	£12.99	Mar
Around Southampton	1-85937-088-8	£12.99	Mar
Around Stratford upon Avon			
	1-85937-098-5	£12.99	Mar
Welsh Castles	1-85937-120-5	£14.99	Mar
Canals and Waterways	1-85937-129-9	£17.99	Apr
East Sussex	1-85937-130-2	£14.99	Apr
Exmoor	1-85937-132-9	£14.99	Apr
Farms and Farming	1-85937-134-5	£17.99	Apr
Around Horsham	1-85937-127-2	£12.99	Apr
Ipswich (pb)	1-85937-133-7	£12.99	Apr
Ireland (pb)	1-85937-181-7	£9.99	Apr
London (pb)	1-85937-183-3	£9.99	Apr
New Forest	1-85937-128-0	£14.99	Apr
Scotland	1-85937-182-5	£9.99	Apr
Stone Circles & Ancient Monuments			
	1-85937-143-4	£17.99	Apr
Sussex (pb)	1-85937-184-1	£9.99	Apr
Colchester (pb)	1-85937-188-4	£8.99	May
County Maps of Britain			
	1-85937-156-6 (192pp)	£19.99	May
Around Harrow	1-85937-141-8	£12.99	May
Leicestershire (pb)	1-85937-185-x	£9.99	May
Lincolnshire	1-85937-135-3	£14.99	May
Around Newquay	1-85937-140-x	£12.99	May
Nottinghamshire (pb)	1-85937-187-6	£9.99	May
Redhill to Reigate	1-85937-137-x	£12.99	May
Scilly Isles	1-85937-136-1	£14.99	May
Victorian & Edwardian Yorkshire			
	1-85937-154-x	£14.99	May
Around Winchester	1-85937-139-6	£12.99	May
Yorkshire (pb)	1-85937-186-8	£9.99	May
Berkshire (pb)	1-85937-191-4	£9.99	Jun
Brighton (pb)	1-85937-192-2	£8.99	Jun
Dartmoor	1-85937-145-0	£14.99	Jun
East London	1-85937-080-2	£14.99	Jun
Glasgow (pb)	1-85937-190-6	£8.99	Jun
Kent (pb)	1-85937-189-2	£9.99	Jun
Victorian & Edwardian Kent			
	1-85937-149-3	£14.99	Jun
North Devon Coast	1-85937-146-9	£14.99	Jun
Peak District	1-85937-100-0	£14.99	Jun
Around Truro	1-85937-147-7	£12.99	Jun
Victorian & Edwardian Maritime Album			
	1-85937-144-2	£14.99	Jun
West Sussex	1-85937-148-5	£14.99	Jun

FRITH PRODUCTS & SERVICES

Francis Frith would doubtless be pleased to know that the pioneering publishing venture he started in 1860 still continues today. More than a hundred and thirty years later, The Francis Frith Collection continues in the same innovative tradition and is now one of the foremost publishers of vintage photographs in the world. Some of the current activities include:

Interior Decoration

Today Frith's photographs can be seen framed and as giant wall murals in thousands of pubs, restaurants, hotels, banks, retail stores and other public buildings throughout the country. In every case they enhance the unique local atmosphere of the places they depict and provide reminders of gentler days in an increasingly busy and frenetic world.

Product Promotions

Frith products have been used by many major companies to promote the sales of their own products or to reinforce their own history and heritage. Brands include Hovis bread, Courage beers, Scots Porage Oats, Colman's mustard, Cadbury's foods, Mellow Birds coffee, Dunhill pipe tobacco, Guinness, and Bulmer's Cider.

Genealogy and Family History

As the interest in family history and roots grows world-wide, more and more people are turning to Frith's photographs of Great Britain for images of the towns, villages and streets where their ancestors lived; and, of course, photographs of the churches and chapels where their ancestors were christened, married and buried are an essential part of every genealogy tree and family album.

A series of easy-to-use CD Roms is planned for publication, and an increasing number of Frith photographs will be able to be viewed on specialist genealogy sites. A growing range of Frith books will be available on CD.

The Internet

Already thousands of Frith photographs can be viewed and purchased on the internet. By the end of the year 2000 some 60,000 Frith photographs will be available on the internet. The number of sites is constantly expanding, each focussing on different products and services from the Collection.

Some of the sites are listed below.

www.townpages.co.uk
www.icollector.com
www.barclaysquare.co.uk
www.cornwall-online.co.uk

For background information on the Collection look at the three following sites:

www.francisfrith.com
www.francisfrith.co.uk
www.frithbook.co.uk

Frith Products

All Frith photographs are available Framed or just as Mounted Prints, and can be ordered from the address below. From time to time other products - Address Books, Calendars, Table Mats, Postcards etc - are available.

The Frith Collectors' Guild

In response to the many customers who enjoy collecting Frith photographs we have created the Frith Collectors' Guild. Members are entitled to a range of benefits, including a regular magazine, special discounts and special limited edition products.

For further information: if you would like further information on any of the above aspects of the Frith business please contact us at the address below:

The Francis Frith Collection, Frith's Barn, Teffont, Salisbury, Wiltshire England SP3 5QP.

Tel: +44 (0) 1722 716 376 Fax: +44 (0) 1722 716 881 Email: uksales@francisfrith.com

To receive your FREE Mounted Print

Cut out this Voucher and return it with your remittance for £1.50 to cover postage and handling. Choose any photograph included in this book. Your SEPIA print will be A4 in size, and mounted in a cream mount with burgundy rule lines, overall size 14 x 11 inches.

Order additional Mounted Prints at HALF PRICE (only £7.49 each*)

If there are further pictures you would like to order, possibly as gifts for friends and family, acquire them at half price (no additional postage and handling required).

Have your Mounted Prints framed*

For an additional £14.95 per print you can have your chosen Mounted Print framed in an elegant polished wood and gilt moulding, overall size 16 x 13 inches (no additional postage and handling required).

> ### * IMPORTANT!
> These special prices are only available if ordered using the original voucher on this page (no copies permitted) and at the same time as your free Mounted Print, for delivery to the same address

Frith Collectors' Guild

From time to time we publish a magazine of news and stories about Frith photographs and further special offers of Frith products. If you would like 12 months FREE membership, please return this form.

Send completed forms to:
The Francis Frith Collection, Frith's Barn, Teffont, Salisbury, Wiltshire SP3 5QP

Voucher for FREE and Reduced Price Frith Prints

Picture no.	Page number	Qty	Mounted @ £7.49	Framed + £14.95	Total Cost
		1	**Free of charge***	£	£
			£	£	£
			£	£	£
			£	£	£
			£	£	£
			£	£	£
			* Post & handling		£1.50

Book Title . . . .   **Total Order Cost** £

Please do not photocopy this voucher. Only the original is valid, so please cut it out and return it to us.

I enclose a cheque / postal order for £ . . . .
made payable to 'The Francis Frith Collection'
OR please debit my Mastercard / Visa / Switch / Amex card

Number . . . .

Expires . . . . Signature . . . .

Name Mr/Mrs/Ms . . . .

Address . . . .

. . . .

. . . .

. . . . Postcode . . . .

Daytime Tel No . . . .   Valid to 31/12/01

The Francis Frith Collectors' Guild

Please enrol me as a member for 12 months free of charge.

Name Mr/Mrs/Ms . . . .

Address . . . .

. . . .

. . . .

. . . . Postcode . . . .

Free Print - see overleaf